r'

Without a Paddle is published under Imagine books, sectionalized division under Di Angelo Publications INC.

IMAGINE BOOKS

an imprint of Di Angelo Publications. Without a Paddle. Copyright 2020. Don Rearden in digital and print distribution in the United States of America.

Di Angelo Publications

4265 San Felipe #1100

Houston, Texas, 77027

www.diangelopublications.com

Library of congress cataloging-in-publications data

Without a Paddle. Downloadable via Kindle, iBooks and NOOK.

Library of Congress Registration

Paperback

ISBN: 978-1-942549-71-0

Layout: Kimberly James

Words by: Don Rearden

1. Poetry

2.Poetry —— Alaska ——United States of America with int. Distribution.

Printed on certified recycled paper.

WITHOUT
A PADDLE

DON REARDEN

Cover Art: *Anesia Travels* by Beth Hill

Table of Contents

déjà vécu 10

Foreign Cold 11

Holy Water 12

Sleepover with a Seal 13

Porch Wolf 14

Headline: State of Alaska 15

My Tarp Coffin 22

Through Alders 24

The Kuskokwim 25

Edwin Wheeler 27

SEE YOU 29

The Honey Bucket Museum 31

Atauciq, Mairuq, Pingayun 32

Weight of a Paper Warrior 35

Portage to the Past 37

A Glacial Goodbye 38

Notice 39

How to Build a Bomb 41

Vitruvian Man 42

VILLAGE SCHOOL BUS 43

Earth Day Sale 44

Caring, On Ice 45

Spring Runoff 45

Magic Carpet Kid 46

For a Day 48

ASSESS THIS 49

After the Marathon Bomber 50

Bake Sale for Big Oil 51

Two Ways to Freeze 52

More Snow Fall 53

Tundra Tapeworm 54

On the Raven Commute 55

Seal Oil Salesman 56

Kim Jong-un: Too Much in the Sun 58

For Dan Bigley   59
ON TODAY'S AGENDA   60
Blue Berry Blue   61
100% Tundra Cotton   62
A Loving Unkindness   63
Musk-Ox Stew, Mexican Beer   64
April Fools' Gold   65
Justice   66
Scars and Claws   67
in the presence of God, dead   69
Growing Seasons   69
No Tremors   70
Drum On   71
Tears for Yuma   73
Fly Forever   74
Like Wedding Guests   75
The Sun Woshippers   76
Somewhere, Florida   77
Armadillo   78
From Left Field   79
You Can Be a Princess, Too   80
The Spaceship Earth Ride   81
RE: Help   82
Marks of a Man   84
Bear Air   85
A Girl Named Pounds   86
Groom Song   87
Old Man in the Tree   88
Without a Paddle   89
New Neighbor Hoods   92
The Raven Hair Girl Who Became   93
    the Sun
dream neighbors   94
On Time   95
the future thins   96
Thunderbirds and Thinking Small   97
Before the Citizens United   99

first kite   100
The Genocide Assignment   101
Bear Aware   102
Lincoln's Chair   103
Old Dog's Turn   104
Dear Son, About That Animal   105
All the Signs Say   106
Nature's Lowest Denominator   107
two sisters strong   108
So Many Aprils   109
Ruling by Fractal   111
Saved by Captain America   112
Return, Raven   113
The Three Year Old at Bedtime   113
Death by Social Media   114
Death by Social Media, 2.0   115
Unbridled Progress   116
Two Hundred Years   117
Field Trip to the Ghost House: 118
    Admit One
This Was   119
Crocodile Killing Walrus   121
Freedom in Chains   122
Coup Counts - for Chief Joe   123
    Medicine Crow
Death by Social Media 3.0   124
Guns in the English Classroom   124
History   125
The Weight of the Immeasurable   127
Like Riding a Bike   127
After ANWR   128
Mosquito   129
Not to Be   130
Simple Sauce   131
Tundra Prom   132
They Say...   133
Before the Avalanche   134

Old Wounds and Flaws   135
SEEK   136
The Rising Leaves   136
Unbecoming Man   137
Earth Day   137
Ghost Ride   138
Tiring   139
Monster Mine   140
Presidential   141
Dog People   143
Shards and Chandeliers   144
On This Day in History   145
Arctic War(n/m)ing   146
Listen and Learn   147
psychopomp (psuchopompos)   149
The Crystal Ball   150
the medicine rises   151
the snow tells stories   152
thinking of you   153
the truth   154
Message Sent   155
On the Fence   156
Dead Horse Trail   157
Missing: Socks   158
Cutting Caribou   159
Today, Refused   159
World of Birds   160
Empty Nest   161
Listen   162
Political Decorum   163
The Shaman Girl   164
Girl Made Climate Change   165
Red Blue   165
This I Miss   166
The Treasure Hunters   167
Lugenpresse   168
Zoom   170

Soothing Souls   170
ESKIMO BASEBALL   171
Spring Change   172
For the Essentials   173
I'm Just Saying   174
Uncertain Endings   175
Last Poem   176

For Alaska and the other three loves of my life:
Annette, Atticus, and Saoirse.

déjà vécu

I've read these headlines before
maybe yesterday, but the date says
otherwise
and that old friend I met today
in her Sorel boots with the gray wool liners
she's the one
the one who told me about you
I remember her saying that before

every other other day someone new dies
someone I knew
and the news doesn't change that much

maybe just the headlines
but I've read them before

and the weather woman flails her arms
at the storm on the map
I've seen her push away the warm before
and this sense

the doctor calls it rare
but he's already said that, too

this disorder
this syndrome disease malady
this sense that I've seen it all before

as I sit at the table
covered in nothing that can surprise me
surrounded and swallowed by
a tomorrow filled with yesterdays

déjà vécu

Foreign Cold

I am not Edward Nelson
explorer, ethnographer, adventurer,
artifact hoarder, preservationist thief
I'm not brave enough to
travel somewhere so foreign cold

a land where people still knew the heft
of a spear
the water repellent beauty of a lightly oiled
seal intestine

I don't have an island in the sea
bearing my name
no collection of Yup'ik artifacts
boxed in my basement

I did not see those bodies
stricken from the maladies of civilization
the whiskeymeaslesmallpoxchristian-flu
absorbed into the tundra sponge
those bodies
"stacked like cordwood"
he wrote in his journal

like cordwood

I could never be Edward Nelson.

Holy Water

They walk on frozen water with
steel chisels and chain saws.

Chips and dust of ice spray
each
cut   chip   chop
closer to safety, salvation, sobriety.

At their feet their work
takes the shape of burden
one long vertical cut
three horizontal slashes
long ---- short / short / long.

Someone will break through
the black will water rise
and the priest will raise
his palms over the whole,

The buckets, cups, pitchers
they fill all
they can carry away.

At the edges of the cross
carved into the river skin
crystals coalesce.

Sleepover with a Seal

I slept beside a seal once
me, on a worn couch
a thin blanket covering

the seal, still frozen
a hundred-mile journey by sled
from a breath hole in the ice
to the painted grey plywood
floor of a house on the tundra

eighth grade, with my mind
on girls and basketball

my parents away and
our apartment in the school
haunted

sleeping at the Slim's
on a worn couch
beside a dead seal

waiting to be transformed

Porch Wolf

barefoot I stepped to the frozen planks
of the porch at night
let the cool soak into my toes
listened to the still of winter dark
reached down to the wood stack
for another piece of fire

brisk steps of another
in the dark, coming around the corner
the flash of a shadow
paws and claws on the same frozen planks
the log drops
with my voice
hey, get the fuck outta here
I yell, as I do the same
reaching, diving for the safety
of a heavy door
the warmth of a woodstove hungry
for another log

Headline: ~~State of~~ Alaska*
(*a catalog of actual headlines from Alaska
Newspapers, 1935 to present)

December 1935
Women Kill Wolf Near Ketchikan

December 1936
Eskimos in Alaska still
leave cherished items
Paddles, Tools, Pots, Pans
on the graves of their dead.

June 1937
Miners Dig Up Story of the Past
conducting searches for minerals
found hundreds of skeletons and skulls
prehistoric mammoths, horses, musk-ox,
wolves, and saber-toothed tigers.

January 1938
In Nichols Bay, 25-Foot Octopus Stalls Boat
small steam launch stalled
octopus attached to the propeller.

October 1939
"Hootch"
a discharged soldier taught them
Indians at Hootznahoo,
the science of distilling liquor.

November 1940
Record Day's Catch
seventy-two seals in one day,

a Prince William Sound Record.
January 1940
A Hanging at Juneau . . . 7th in Alaska
thirty-seven-year-old Indian,
paid the supreme penalty
for killing his mother-in-law in a drunken rage.

May 1941
Recent Census
results
population at 72,524.

February 1942
Wartime Blackouts
Cities practice
several hours of the night.

June 1942
Japanese
        Bomb
            Dutch
            Harbor.

May 1943
Eskimo Troops Aid War Effort
modern rifles instead of spears,
Eskimo troops act
as scouts and lookouts.

June 1944
Aleut Children Spurn Candy for War Stamps
The storekeeper at the evacuation colony
Says he stocks war stamps

Instead of candy
to keep the young Aleut customers happy.
June 1945
Barrow's First Talkies Flown in by Army
An Eskimo woman watched
scantily clad women dance for the first time
"Now we know why our store is always short of cloth.
People outside must be really hard up for cloth!"

March 1946
POWs Choose Atka
Twenty-five Attu Aleuts
survive Japanese imprisonment, decide against returning
home,
choose to live on Atka.

1946
Navy Pushes Barrow Oil Search...Early Results Encouraging

There's Lumber in Wrangell's Future

1947-----------Pork Chops, Whisky, Cheer Stranded
Flyer. Fur Rich Natives on Spending Spree. Voters of
Statehood . . . 9625 to 6822. First Woman to Climb
McKinley. Eskimo Hunter Surprised from Behind.

1948
94,000 Civilians
in Alaska
Now.

1949
Trapped Behind Iron Curtain...Alaskan Eskimos
Held for Two Months. Raging River Relents. 17 Days

Adrift on Bering Strait Ice Floes. It's All-out
War Against Wolf, Coyote. Air Force Bombs
Ice-Choked Interior Rivers. Wolf Bounty Now
$50.
Man Stabs, Kills Bear.

April, 1950.

Ingenius Eskimo Repairs His Own Watch.

March, 1950.
Inventive Indian Masters Balky Motor

1959
WE'RE IN!
VOTE MAKES ALASKA
49th STATE

1960
Oil Biggest Well Yet.

$4 Million Oil Leases. The 'Iron Dog'. . . A
Threat to Alaska's Historic Dog Team. Death
of a Dog Musher. Grizzly Wrecks Plane. 118
Rural Schools. Fierce Gales, Mountainous
Seas...Boats Lost...Three Sailors Missing.
Perils of the Hunt...Walrus Attacks Boat.
Whaling Fleet Idled.

Skookum Jim's Legacy

She Recalls First Whites to Visit Her People

Man Eating Sharks Invade Southeast Alaska.

Free Farm Land for the Asking?

Ice Box for Eskimos

Gas Find. Major Oil Find. Milestone for Oil.
Big Tonnage Gain for Anchorage. Oil Well in
Cook Inlet Fuels 14-month Fire.

1964

Eskimo Chiefs Convene

First Bank Robbery

Boom in Oil Drilling.

EARTHQUAKE!

1965. 67. 69. 70.
Alaskan Totems – Heritage in Peril. Live Net-
work TV for Southeast Soon. Pipeline Project
Bogs Down. Alaska Grows.
        Highest Pay.
        High Bids For Land.
        Alaskan Boating Deaths
        Exceed National Average.

1974

Law Okays the Pipeline,
Cost Spirals to $4.5 Billion

Cash for Natives

PIPELINE WORK BEGINS

Four Year University for Barrow this Fall

TV for Eskimos Good News and Bad News
1985.
State Mistakes Cost Millions: Native Corporation
Got Oil, Gas Worth $500 Million

March 25, 1989.
VALDEZ SPILL CRUDE OIL FOULS SOUND
LARGEST EVER IN U.S.

1991.
War Touches Banks of Remote Kobuk River.
Alaskan Falls in Battle.
Soldotna Man, a father-to-be,
Killed in Action.

1992.
HIGH BIRTH RATE BOOSTS ALASKA
POPULATION 587,000
ANCHORAGE, 240,258.

1997.
Group Appeals to Halt Timber Sale, Says it Threatens Birds.
State Doctors Told to Watch
for Bird Flu.

Alaskans Prepare for 2000 Census.

Pipeline Shooting Trial Set in Fairbanks, 2001.

ANWR's Dead, Say all Sides, 2002.

                    2003.   2004.
Suicide Strikes Village.
        Alaskans At War.
                Drilling Plans Irk Native Whalers.
Alaskan Guard Heads to Kosovo. Leaving for Iraq.
National Guard Troops Depart for Training and
Middle East. Japanese War Planes Return to Alas-
kan Skies. Anti-terror Unit Comes to Anchorage.

Wounded Alaskan Recovers.

    Saving Ourselves.   Urban Bear Attack.

    Save Yourself.   Bears' Attack Kills Eagles.

    Oasis of Hope.
        Bear Attacks Lead Officials to Ban
        Fishing at Night.

~~Wildflowers with the Natives~~
    ~~Plant with the Native Society~~
        ~~Plant Society with the Native~~
    ~~Celebrate the Native Plants~~
~~Natives Celebrate. Wildflower Celebrates. Wild-~~
~~flowers with Natives Celebrate Society. Society~~
~~Celebrates. Natives Celebrate Society. Native~~
~~Society.~~
~~Society Celebrates Wildflower Plants with Natives.~~

Celebrate Wildflowers with the Native Plant Society

My Tarp Coffin

With a jump I awoke
and in the tempest
my heart broke,
and with the tent sank
into the darkness
of the lake.

All alone, but still alive
shivering, struggling, to survive
with a tarp
my coffin made
and in the screaming wind
I stayed.

From the mountain sky
torrential rain –
muscle quivers
giving way to pain
and finally, the morning ray
blowing in
the frigid day.

From the cold cocoon I came
drenched and weary
from the rain.
Into the brush,
with tarp and knife
to build a fire …
for my life.

Creeping cold
caressed my soul,
the sleepless night was
taking toll
and finally, a twig alighted
a chance, a hope -
when flame ignited.

As the wind and rain raged
a separate battle had been waged
and from the brush a victor strode
warm and strong against the cold,
with the flames devoured fear
and finally, the sky would clear –
for a peek, the shore I neared,
where my tent had disappeared.

Through Alders

where the alders arch low

passage to a place
impossible tunnels
a maze
low hanging trail
somewhere the golden leaf carpet
stirs, rustles
with the heart
a flash of adrenaline
through arteries that snake
like paths through alders

where bear move
without sound

The Kuskokwim

this river began
ak'a tamanii
a long time ago
and to those who lived along
this river's banks, and those
who dipped paddles, nets, and boat bows
this river meant life

and even now,
in times of crashing ice
and turning tide
this river brings hope
this river gives
this river takes

and from here,
this river has no end

this river flows and oxbows
and churns and turns in impossible
directions

like a tundra swan's neck
this river
curves back upon itself

an endless series
of question marks
that never question

this river was here before us
and will forever flow
into the horizon

and those who choose
to make their home
along the banks
this river is life

Edwin Wheeler

The Edwin I knew
stole bikes in Bethel
rode them to rust
in the tundra dust
then stacked frames, rims, seats
and flattened tire tubes
in a sepulchral pile
beside the plywood box shanty
that was his home

My dad, his probation officer,
called him "the runner"
and that is what he did
when people began to wrap
chains around their cycles
he Ran booze for bootleggers
dope for dealers

Edwin moved to Anchorage
like many of us and
I hope before he died
homeless
alone
he snatched
at least one hillside ride, maybe
a sweet Cannondale, tricked out
full suspension, hydraulic disc brakes, a ding
ding bell

I hope they let Edwin
into heaven so he can
 ride the hell
out of the gold paved
streets behind the pearly gates

And when he's done
ditch God's bike
in the long grass
beside a salmon stream

SEE YOU

I've never been good
at good - byes

I prefer the Yup'ik tradition
piur'aa : stay as you are
or just "See You."

it's not as final
those two words don't squeeze
at the heart
like good-bye

there I am, ready
to make tracks to Alaska
to see my friends and family
to again join the people who say,
"See You."

But right now I am in the land of good-byes
and it is good-bye
that even a "piur'aa" cannot cover

You are there on the couch
and you rise
not like a man who is waning
from cancer
but like Marcus Allen in his prime
---just tackled in the end zone ---
touchdown.

I throw my arms around you
I feel your bones
you hold me with
the last of your strength
and this is the last time.
We both know it.

I savor your warmth,
hoping I will never forget
your smile, your smell, your love
and I fight the tears
I don't know what it means
to be good at saying
good-bye
but I did my best Grandpa

see you.

The Honey Bucket Museum

politicians stood with suited smiles
pumping hands, holding giant scissors
a red ribbon waved in the wind

the buckets weren't gone
but that didn't matter

the museum couldn't wait any longer

democracy finally worked, mostly
like it had for the Romans
thousands of years earlier,
flowing like their ancient waterworks
a few sweet government contracts

these were the men who plumbed Prudhoe
no task too small, mostly

the buckets weren't gone
but that didn't matter

there were ribbons that needed cutting

Atauciq, Malruq, Pingayun

One: Atauciq
Cup'aq rides on her mother's back
down the slippery boardwalk
past the curled and snoozing sled dogs
towards her head start on life

the magical building
unlike anywhere in the village
with little tables and chairs made just for her
fingerpaints, shelves of colorful books, a toy
kitchen

how many boats can you count?
her mother asks
Cup'aq stretches a blue knitted mitten
to the morning mirror of the bay
counts:

Atuaciq, Malruq, Pingayun
she says

now kass'atun
her mother says

One, Two, Three
Cup'aq says.

Two: Malruq
Isaac's son was shy at first
but the cook took him
under her wing and now
each night he talks about how

he set up tables for lunch
painted muskox, ducks, and seals
with his fingers

sometimes Isaac hears him
singing the Yup'ik alphabet song
and, when they walk together to school
in the morning dark

the snow diamonds sparkling
in the flashlight's glow
he remembers his own father
walking him through the village
braving the monster-filled shadows

bundled back then in his little squirrel-lined parka
the thick warm hood drawn tight to keep out
the wind

Isaac wonders if his son will someday
make the same walk
with a son of his own
if their stories of hunting and school
still told in the tongue of their ancestors.

Three: Pingayun
Cup'aq's brown eyes turn down
where her oldest two daughters,
clench crayons and shifting snow white
pages into worlds of color

33

she carries her third,
on her hip into the kitchen
who wants to make necklaces?
she asks, carrying a flat cake pan
filled with dyed Cheerios
red, plain, and blue

she made her own jewelry once
slipping string through the cereal holes
fine tuning motor skills, learning
the months and days, and how to brush baby teeth
wash dirty hands

now, a world away from the Bering Sea
and the village she called home
she tries to recreate that magic
of learning and excitement
for her own daughters

they count the little cereal gems
in Yup'ik: Atauciq, Malruq, Pingayun

Weight of a Paper Warrior

I sit on the carpeted classroom floor
encircled
Tlingit, Haida, Aleut, Yup'ik, Inupiaq, Athabascan
city boys
I wear my Raven qaspeq
hand sewn with love by a Yup'ik friend

they close their eyes
the walls around us, and that separate
fall away
my words carry them back in time
to when they were warriors

when they fought for what they believed
to protect their families, their people
to survive

this warrior is still there, I say

in you

listen to him

these were his

a stone knife, an arrowhead, a rabbit bone charm
travel — small hand to small hand around the
circle
for some cool trinkets, for others
a weight to each I will never know

the circle breaks and they lie on sheets
of white butcher paper, draw Crayola silhouettes
then arm and illustrate

one boy tells me:
my spirit warrior's knife
was different and sharper
and
he said he will always
be there when I am scared

another asks:
what did your spirit warrior
look like?

this little boy's question lingers and
I am suddenly naked

Portage to the Past

pulled and polled towards the pass
huffing and puffing, squinting in the sun
this portage used by the Real People

imagined that I was not pulling my child
in a pulk of plastic, synthetic,
refined metal

instead he rides in the wood
and hide frame on my back

babiche and birch snowshoes
not Rossignol and Swix
moose and caribou
for Smartwool and GoreTex

at the base of the last step
we turned back
too steep to continue

thwarted by fear
disinclined by the incline
no inclination to pass the pass

there would be no portage for us

a portage to a different land
a portage to the past

A Glacial Goodbye

your mother carried you
on skis
to this glacier
a month before you were born
I pulled you here
in a sled
a month before your first birthday
we've brought you here again
a month before the second
our new family tradition

each time you are older, bigger
each time this ancient glacier
smaller
melting, crackling, splintering, calving

I fear someday it will not be here
for you to bring your family
but more than that
I fear the day I won't be

Notice

I enter the double doors to this campus building
daily, ignoring the bold black and red decal
NOTICE!
the one on every door on every building

at this place of learning

two simple symbols
a red circle with a line through
a black pistol

several of the scopes
locked in my safe at home
look like this circle
quarter turn clockwise, swap red to black
add an extra black line
cross-hairs
on every door on every building
at this place of learning
this is not how you teach
this is not best practices
this solves nothing

there should instead be signs
reminders, really
NOTICE!
and just the circle
inside the circle:
books, figures holding hands, smiles,
people thinking, loving, learning, living.

NOTICE!

on every door, on every building
at this place of learning

How to Build a Bomb

add two parts oppression
blend sadness, loneliness, fear
a dash of ignorance
mix in hubris, egotism, vanity

bring to boil
broil, blacken
let cook
bake covered
bake uncovered
let cool

pour into pressure cooker
sprinkle with terror
garnish with counter-terror

turn on high

Vitruvian Man

suddenly,
you are the Vitruvian Man, mid-air
flying over the handlebars

of a mountainbike
twenty-five miles an hour
winding narrow paved Flourentine road

certain disaster
just as the man Davinci convinced
to fly in his crazy craft,
from that wine and olive-grove hillside
you will be a crumble wreck of a corpse

but what should have been
bones and blood
instead two quarter sized burns
above the knees
road rash, a torn fingernail
a bike bent and broken

the culprit, a camera
clattering down the concrete

somehow, strangely, you are standing
on your feet
a Vitruvian man

VILLAGE SCHOOL BUS

in August, the school bus arrived
a giant aluminum boat
we piled in, half a village
of children, grinning
into the brisk morning air

October ice, freeze-up
found me stuck
on the other side
ice-pans keeping the bus
from delivering us home
on the river road

no relatives to stay with
Wilson's family took me in
slept on the floor
beside his bed
ate blackfish, dried pike, white fish
salmon strips, seal oil
charged the occasional frozen
pizza to my dad's account
at the village store
maybe a few extra corn-nuts
and blackcherry Shasta

when the river froze
the bus arrived
to take us home

a giant wooden sled

Earth Day Sale

in our culture we find
one day to honor those things
we say we love most
one for
our mothers
our fathers
our leaders
our genocidal explorers

create cards
hallmarks for a single day
parade
send roses
buy candy
close banks
find empty mailboxes
        waiting for cards
from the other days we circle the sun

Caring, On Ice

stand at the face
of a glacier
stare into those
crevasses of time
wrinkles around
Mother Earth's eyes

and tell me again
her tears
matter not

Spring Runoff

today I am an icicle
on the eave, the edge
melting in the warm
winnowing away
clinging to a fragment
of winter while
above, the blue beyond
and I cannot runoff

Magic Carpet Kid

you float into my office
as if on a magic carpet
heading to Arizona, coach
you tell me
going to learn to fly helicopters, coach
you say
grin as wide as a rotor swath

over a decade ago
after a sleepless night
on cold hard village school floor
I drew impossible black lines on a clipboard
overtime out of reach, my first loss looms
seven seconds left
down by four
we can win this, coach
you said

more impossible lines
you were the X
inbound from the baseline
find the far left corner
skip pass back to your X
 X makes the three — then trap
on the made – steal, shoot
make it
get fouled
make it

and you do

you ---float
as if on a magic carpet

and we are lifted
seeing in you
what is possible for us all

For a Day

AfterCrisisWeConverge
becomeONEagain

for a day

become kind and care

for   a   day

the   next   it   begins
                      again, the soured divide

                         but

for a day

we converge

if only
                         for a day

ASSESS THIS

we sit in a circle
as our ancestors

this is real learning
she says
but in school
its all memorization and tests
and you forget afterwards

just like how we forgot
the circle
isn't only to be darkened
with a #2 pencil

After the Marathon Bomber

1. On your mark
2. Get set
3. Go
4. Start slow
5. Don't get caught
6. In the excitement
7. You'll burn out
8. All the others
9. Think about them, the finish line
10. Run your own race
11. Set your own pace
12. Not even half way yet
13. Or now
14. Finally, midway
15. Begin to hurt, bleed
16. Drink more
17. Avoid cramping
18. Blisters
19. Prepare for
20. The Pain
21. The Wall
22. It's here
23. Or here.
24. You want to die
25. But you push through
26. Triumph over the terror
26.2 And keep running

Bake Sale for Big Oil

for his was a brilliant plan
as their leader he knew
they needed him to do
something big

for their problems
big
enormous, like their state

honey buckets, tuberculosis
a contagion of self-slaughter
domestic violence, homelessness
needles, pills, empty bottles

so many problems
big
must be his action

he got started immediately
putting together all the ingredients
mixing, setting the oven's temp

soon the timer chimed

bake sale for big oil

Two Ways to Freeze

old cabin
hidden in the spindly spruce
boarded windows
moose antler handle door
irony freezer
to ski to your porch
in the blinding sun of spring
is one thing
to stumble upon you
in the dark of winter
freezing fear, another

More Snow Fall

through waist deep snow
I carry you on my shoulders
you sing about the old farmer
and yell, "Tree! Tree!"
at each hemlock we pass

I struggle with every step
wading, post-holing, breath
exploding from my mouth
white plumes you reach
for with your black mittens
"Hot Hot!" you cheer

my foot drops without warning
the culprit an old moose hoof
punched even deeper
we tumble forward
I lift you off my shoulder
as we fall, turning your face
towards the brilliant blue above

for a moment, dead still
staring up at the sky
snow fills the hole around our faces
I worry you are scared
or worse, hurt
but then you giggle, and ask
"More? More?"

I won't be there to always
catch you when you fall,
but I will always fall with you
and be there when you're ready
for more

Tundra Tapeworm

like a tapeworm
these rivers attach
themselves to your insides

when you can peer out
from your exit row
at 20,000 feet and know
one bend from the next

you are infected

these twists and turns
burned into your brain
the arteries and veins
of your life

there is no cure
for this malady
no stick to wrap the worm
and twist it from your guts
a half turn a day forever

On the Raven Commute

they head to work in the morning
as we do
but they fly, swoop and play, together
we drive
stare ahead without emotion

at days end they commute
as we do
towards home, rolling and cackling, together
we drive
stare ahead without emotion

we could learn a thing or two,
together
like we once did

Seal Oil Salesman

Step right up and dip your:

Salmon! Pike! Whitefish! Blackfish!
Lushfish! Halibut!

For all fish:
Dried, smoked, baked, frozen,
fermented, and raw!

Ingest for:
Stomach ache! Constipation! Diarrhea!
Body aches, cold, flu, general malaise!

For Eskimo Ice-Cream mix with:
A splash of boiling water, Crisco,
whip with your bare hand
add sugar
salmon berries, blue berries, and crow!

Rub on:
Frost bite, burns, sore joints!
Cheeks! Lips! Wounds!

Use for:
Waterproofing, lubrication, softening!
Heat, light, and warmth!

Does not:
emit carbon, pollute, cause wars

Does not:
ruin beaches, rivers, lakes, oceans

Does not:
cause cancer, greed, avarice
Does not:
require pipelines, drilling, corruption

Step right up!

Kim Jong-un: Too Much in the Sun

his soldiers march in comical precision
punching the air like a million Mike Tysons

they parade giant missiles through town
on the nightly news we see maps
drawn with concentric circles
told not to worry

his nukes can only hit
Hawaii
or
Alaska

but when they call him crazy
I can't help but think of another son
who lost his father
and that mousetrap did not end well

For Dan Bigley

in a flash
the world gone black

the culprit
a brown blur of brawn

the bear's eyes
the last your own
will ever see

all hope
would seem lost
in the darkness

and yet you
become the sun
and show us all
how to see

beyond our own
bears

ON TODAY'S AGENDA

1. Second and call the Question
2. Discuss. Discuss. Discuss.
3. No order to the points.
4. Please no point of clarification.
5. No moves to entertain.
6. Favor all those
7. Unanimous and
8. Someone please motion to adjourn
9. This death by agenda

Blue Berry Blue

a white Styrofoam™ cup
filled to the rim with tundra
blue berries
just picked, the skin
of each a light soft blue,
and just beneath the surface
a deeper blue, a darkness

not unlike the bruises
often found on the very
Alaskan women who pick
these sweet berries
their numbers, like the contents
in the cup, beyond count

and our leaders argue over oil
focused only on filling the pipeline
with the darkness
needed to manufacture the cup
and they continue
to ignore the contents

100% Tundra Cotton

I want them to discover
the value of tundra cotton
swaying in the breeze
plump blue berries
moose and salmon
spiders, furry yellow caterpillars
mosquitos and even no-see-ums

I want them to know
a crane call from a loon's cry
the difference between a
rainbow and a sundog

I want them to imagine
gold deposits beneath
their favorite park
an oil well under
their swimming pool

A Loving Unkindness

last year I doubted
your choice for a home
Seuss-like spruce
spindly, impossibly tall
unprotected from the williwaw winds
that whip and turn trees
in this valley
into toothpicks

the stickhouse endured, your loving unkindness
survived, narrowly
one of your coal black youth
flew like Davinci's craft
busted a leg, landing instead
at the avian hospital,
thanks to a human neighbor

now you are back. Rebuilding.
flight after flight, with just
the right branch of hemlock,spruce, birch
you work together throughout
day after day, crafting a home
built to survive hurricane gusts
you prepare for new lives
eggs, then hungry mouths
open toward the sky, waiting

and I will not doubt you again
as I chose this mountain valley
for my nest,
too.

Musk-Ox Stew, Mexican Beer

Seth and I made camp at the edge of the earth
amid the white bones of a whale
and the grey skeleton of an old skiff

we collected driftwood, set ablaze with dried moss
a splash of dinosaur
wolfed down the fire warmed muskox stew
in gloved hands, sipped half slushed Tecate,
cut slices of frozen lime with a Leatherman

the cold war sun slipped beneath the sea
a submarine bound for the gulags,

a frigid black sky followed
we gathered more sticks, more moss
hunched closer to the blaze
surrounded by waves, wind, and bears

we told stories, laughed, and spoke of nothing
and everything

as if this had always been
and would always be

then like gasoline on water,
the colors slid across the surface of the sky
ignited, and bathed the edge of the earth
in the icy light of Aurora's warmth

April Fools' Gold

We dig until our fingers bleed
until mountains become gaping holes
visible from space
rivers run the color of rust
flavored with arsenic
for the fish and fowl

we lust for the luster
shimmy for the shine
hammer out thin coats
to cover our dead and divine
those poor prophets
we have enshrined
in gold

the very object of our worship

and yet

we fool no one, but ourselves.

Justice

today I worry
justice is not blind
perhaps at night
after the gavel drops
she removes the kerchief
from her brow
sets the scales aside

does she dine downtown
on the DA's dime? or
sip fine white wine
in a dark corner
of a smoky dive
where the sign reads:

> *check your sword*
> *at the bar*

today I worry not
that she can see
but she hears
knows
the jingle of pennies
from bullion

today I worry
while she's away
in the darkness of
our hallowed halls
someone fiddles with
the beam and balance

Scars and Claws

the black cat
on my chest
makes me work
for each breath
her sandpaper tongue
scales at my fingers
seven pounds
of scars and claws
press down

the soft rumble of her
purr reminds ---
for all that haunts me
troubles my sleep
keeps me from myself ---
  I must take
another breath

in the presence of God, dead

raven
rumpled black
in the snow
this vision
haunts me still

creator
now dead
power lost
long before a wing
clipped the wires
--the new power--
hanging over the land

sometimes I still stand
over the ruffled coal corpse
the cold sears my cheeks
I blink ice
and wonder what one
should do
in the presence of God,
dead and
I cannot bury him
in the crusty white
covering the tundra

Growing Seasons

my saw blade reveals
the concentric rings
of a tree
ring inside of ring
spruce inside of spruce
cracks open from the bark
point towards the core
where it all started
the first year

of the hundred or so
the good seasons standout
and the rough years
wear thin,
like people

but when we are cut down
when cracks run toward
our center
there are no rings
no circles, no clear picture
to mark the number
of winters we stood
before the final fire

No Tremors

tremors shook Rome today
not far from the coliseum
and from the rubble and screams
came a corpse count
of ten score and more

tragedy shook the rubble
of Detroit today
and in their dome
70,000 screams
at the score
but no tremors
at the thought
if their coliseum
could endure the collapse

Drum On

(in memoriam: Chris Morgan)

go today, and
steam bend birch
twice the length of your leg
to form a perfect circle
add a handle, now
cover with a seal skin
carve a narrow drumstick
elbow to fingertips

begin to tap lightly
allow the rhythm
to become the drum
within us
the heart renewed

drum on

share this ancestral gift
the cycle of stick and skin
remind us how each beat
needs the one before
and after
how rhythm without
the drummer
is life without breath
a silence not meant
for man

begin to tap lightly
allow the rhythm
to become the drum
within us
the heart renewed
a heart anew

drum on

Tears for Yuma

tears
when news of her death
came in short words
manly words between
two men mourning
the death of a dog

tears for Yuma

and yet
when the thin sounds
of sadness slice the ice,
snow, mountains, separating me
from my tundra home
friends, family, and you
crashing river ice
yellow nylon ropes
wound round necks
shotgun shells and churchbells
overdose and comatose
drowned and found
in waters of sorrow
eyes frozen open
in fear

and yet,
I shed not
a solitary
  tear
save for Yuma

Fly Forever
(in memoriam: Seth Fairbanks)

go today
touch your tundra tires
to a gravel bar
dip your wings to the wolves
a bear, a moose, the caribou
fly perfect circles,
in the midnight sun
fear nothing

be restless, only with stillness
like the Kuskokwim,
always in motion
always churning, turning
humor twisted
lips uplifted flaps
in a perpetual grin

fly forever

remind us how to soar
how flight without
the pilot
is life without love
an existence not meant
for man
allow the rhythm of
the cub's hum
to become the drum
within us
our hearts, now in two
renewed
until one day we
will fly too

fly forever

Like Wedding Guests

Petals in the sand
recycled rings exchanged
pelicans floating through
the azure uninvited but welcome
brown and white
tanned and burned listen
as the waves kiss the shore
all just grains of silica
a single moment solidified
the water retreats
like wedding guests
from the reception
after the last song

The Sun Worshippers

they turn their faces
burned red white
blacked baked braised
toward the sky
they bare their
flesh, oiled and wanting
sacrificing, enticing
the great golden orb
overhead to bless them
with beauty
with skin the color
of those ancient men
the sun worshippers
the ignorant pagans
and their false prophets and
pyramids to the sun

Somewhere, Florida

three at the buffet
load plates
heaping piles, barbecue ribs
fried chicken, crab Rangoon
honey chicken, pork fried rice

they are serious about this
All-You-Can-Eat-Lunch
no words, no smiles
the white dinner plate
disappears
beneath a growing mound
of despair
I can hear their bellies bulge
before the food ever
touches their lips
and I set my own
sad fork aside

Armadillo

at dusk my first armadillo
runs for his life
I park the car
my eyes catch movement
like they would at home for

lynx coyote owl
I should follow him
study him
tell him I am sorry
about what they have
done to his home
the swimming pool houses

the sunburned tourists
safe inside their rented shells

From Left Field

I will never make
as much money
as the man on first

second owns a yacht
the size of my house

the diamond stud in third's ear
I can see from left field
it shines in the artificial sunlight

at the smack crack of leather
on wood a white blurrrrr
bounces past the shortstop
with the underwear ads

toward center and his dance club

and I am left to wonder
if right has a charity
or if he sends money
to Havana, sewn
inside shirts with his
name embroidered
on the back

You can be a Princess, too

at breakfast
they announce your name
in small squeaky voices
a flock of handpicked
doves to tell you
what you want to hear
over eggs and bacon
a queen's feast,
with fresh squeezed Florida

you can be a princess, too
and for the rest of the day
and your magic kingdom lifetime
you will remind them

The Spaceship Earth Ride

inside Spaceship Earth
you crawl past cavemen
and their crude portraits
of mammoth hunts
"This is primitive man"
the voice from above says
and his biggest fault
rested in his immobile paintings

then comes the pyramid builders
with their papyrus plans
then moveable type
telegrams to radio programs
televised moon landings
warehouse sized computers
and man is advancing
with technological wonders
that are out of this world

which is just where you will
want to live
when man is finished with
The Spaceship Earth ride

RE: Help

her subject line says:
help

then:
as you've known
I've been facing family
and personal problems
in my head---

her words and
now, in my own head
flashbacks of students past
lost to self-slaughter

I don't want to lose faith
in life altogether

she says

she falls further and further

twice she repeats this
further and further

into depression

depression
further she falls

And fuck school

she says
adding she hates how
she feels and the things she
says

And fuck everything

But I don't like the thoughts
I'm thinking

she says this and I
don't like the thoughts
either

help

her subject line says
demolishing my heart with:

So please
I greatly need it

those were not her final words

not all cries for help go unanswered

not all endings here are sad

Marks of a Man

thin sheen of crystal
covers the gravel road
running beneath, clear
cold water
why am I suddenly thirsty?
these boots break through
slim shards crack
crumble and mix
mud washes away
all that was meaningful
  my mouth loses interest
in sipping spring
so I crunch away
and behind leave
lonely murky marks
of a man

Bear Air

the sour air
a bear
fresh from
his den
a skunk would shrink in shame
but there are no
skunks in the last frontier
so suddenly
the stench ignites
primal neurons
raises neck hairs
the foul air
like some ghostly specter
in the dark of the woods
he is here
or was there, here
no matter
the smell lingers
surrounds and
mixes with the fear

A Girl Named Pounds

four hundred fifty reasons
why you should enjoy
another movie
another song
and sing along

four hundred and fifty reasons
you should pop your head
into my office doorway
and say --- *hey Don*

four hundred and fifty reasons
why at age twelve
you should have known
the love of a mother
who would fill you
with confidence not cake

forsake and forgive
those who laughed
poked, taunted and teased
they now bear the weight
and great burden
of four hundred fifty excuses

Groom Song

a tear hits
the groom's guitar
he strums the strings,
the rings in place
the priest's soft smile
(the Uncle's guile)
all the while
he sings
she cries
his own eyes tear
his fear that the words
would not come, some
  scrawl of lyrics
taped to the top
of the guitar
by far, will make
the icing on this
wedding cake

Old Man in the Tree

outside in the tree
I see a face
old man's visage
eyes of twisted
birch branches
framed black against
the blue night sky
his nose grows green
with summer sun

sometimes snow droops heavy
on his branches
and he smiles

Without a Paddle

the motor sputtered a lifetime away from the
village
John lifted the gas tank
into the blue sky with one swift jerk
empty

no current to carry us home

across the shallow lakes
down the winding river

no wind to blow away
the growing fog of buzzing vampires

the fourteen feet of aluminum boat
carried only the following:
one 8th grade whiteboy in hip boots
one 10th grade Yupik bird hunting machine
two shotguns
several dead ducks (various species)
one empty red gas tank
one silver anchor with yellow rope

missing:
gas, oar, radio

we knew this much:
no one would look for us
no one would worry about us
until several hours after dark
and that was a month away

we also knew this much:
we had to save ourselves
or get lucky and hope
for other hunters

we didn't get lucky

I stuffed my Remington
barrel first into my hip boot
and began to paddle

John threw out the anchor
towards home
and began to pull in the line

the shotgun paddle didn't work
I removed the outboard engine cover
and scooped singing

row row the boat

progress came an arm-length
and anchor throw at a time

hungry and thirsty
we stopped and devoured
tundra blackberries
drank the murky water

throw, pull, paddle
paddle, pull, throw

the sun circled the Arctic
and threatened to return
home still not even
on the watery horizon

our stomach's ached
but we laughed,
told stories

we would get home eventually
mosquito bitten and tired
and would never forget
to check the fuel

or how an anchor

is nothing until

it is everything

New Neighbor Hoods

the valley clamor quieted
when the merlins swooped
into the neighborhood
like flying bandits
boomerang shaped raptors
zipping through the hemlock
under stripes black against the azure sky

even the largest of the songbirds
the ruling raven couple sat stoic
on a spruce top
their dark stare contempt
as the invading immigrants
laid claim to their old home
just a couple trees over
from the new nest

there would be no friendly welcome
no apple pies or fresh cookies
just cold stillness
the chatter of the two falcons
an unwelcome car alarm
in a place where they

had never locked the doors

The Raven Hair Girl Who Became the Sun

(for Dakota)

the dust of stars

is within us all

they say, but your eyes

sparkled a slice of sun

and now on raven wings

may you fly

and return to us

as the sun each day

dream neighbors

I visited their house
the neighbors
they were gone
I was bringing a spare bed
tucked in a small box
a neighborly gift
I waited at the door
then shoveled moose shit
around their yard
and when the owner
arrived he was angry
but for those dreamlike
reasons that make sense
only while asleep

concern, he voiced
my old dog might add
to the moose droppings
and I promised
to shovel any piles
like a good neighbor

then I realized
I had been there before
to that house
talking with neighbors
who exist only in my dreams

On Time

on time, they say
time goes faster
with time and there isn't
enough time in the day
just in time, this time
and you don't know
the time of day
before your time
because time

is valuable
is money
is now

about time
there isn't enough
time on your side
when it's time
to go

the future thins

the future thins
when the ice begins
to crack beneath us
glass spider webs
appear under our soles
cold black below
we slow but keep on track
never looking back

Thunderbirds and Thinking Small

Kevin sends me a photo
he knows I will love
the two of us have
whittled away many summer suns
speaking of these creatures
the monsters of his culture

the creature that appears
on my phone, in my hand
ancient Yup'ik art on seal gut

imagine, I reply
---- digital smoke signals
ones and zeroes across infinite mountains ---
what it was like
birds that could carry away
caribou, a whale
a hunter in his kayak

funny how we never hear about the raptors
in the time of mega-fauna
soaring above mammoth carcasses
snarling scimitar cats, cave bears, dire wolves

I picture them, these enormous avians
feathered Cessnas, with harpoon talons

Kevin brings me back to earth,
to our time, and with his joke
reminds me how my whiteboy brain
has much to learn:

*Or maybe we're thinking
in the wrong direction
maybe it's a miniature
caribou roaming the
tundra, small enough to
be eaten by ptarmigan.*

Before the Citizens United

actually they didn't abolish Pre-K
like everyone said they would
they just renamed it
and everyone could go
even the poor and non-white
children, the non-Christian, too

Lego, then Mattel, Fisher-Price
Parker Bros, X-Box, Apple
the new levels for school
and each school a new name,
based upon the sponsor

Martin Luther Exxon Elementary
George Washington Koch Middle
Thomas Jefferson Boeing High

redesigned curriculum:
growth, profit, history's mysteries
intelligent design, marketing
religion, constitution, husbands
and wives, science fictions

the jails and the colleges followed suit,
suits were required,
even the lawsuits didn't last long
the courts had sponsors, too

the citizens united, in anger
but the rebellion lasted only a day
there were shows to watch, games
to cheer, and beer

oh, the beer

first kite

swirling storm gusts
and you race
between us
in your little rubber
boots across the field
thin white line into the sky
crappy plastic kite
collapsing upon itself
with each blast of wind

but it flies and you cackle
running wide loops

above the thin flat bird
with the streaming blue tail
two hawks circle

above our laughter
but not our love

This Genocide Assignment

Professor Don,

said a note
at the bottom
of an essay

this genocide assignment
haunted me

followed by a question:

did you give us this topic
just for a grade,
or something more?

Beneath her grade

I wrote:

something more,
young scholar
something more

Bear Aware

they know not what they do
dump piles of tasty morsels
perfectly fine food
in barrels before breakfast

waste while we watch
wait, weary of the wind
that bears their scent

their piles of hunger
draw us despite danger
anger at our instict
to taste, not waste

and we will pay, because
they know not what they do

Lincoln's Chair

the red on this chair
from a nation divided
contempt for change
shot from a derringer
a dagger slash
fear on the balcony
the stage set
acts upon acts
players and plays
crimson playbills
mutter "useless" last lines
and exit
stage left
empty as a blood
and brain stained chair

Old Dog's Turn

a stopwatch hand
the old dog moves
in a circle, claws clicking
turns again, again
we watch him spin

canine evolution or
trampling down invisible grass
on a wood floor

furry turntable
black and white wheel
breathing merry-go-round

each revolution
one of his fifteen years
two seconds per rotation
paws ticking away
this time we all have left

Dear Son, About that Animal

Dear Son,

I'm sorry I didn't do more
but I didn't know it was so bad
let me try again

I'm sorry I didn't do anything
but there wasn't anything I could do
let me try again

I'm sorry I couldn't stop it
but they were so far away
let me try again

I'm sorry I didn't fight
but I was so busy
let me try again

I'm sorry I did nothing
but I wasn't alone
let me try again

I'm sorry we did nothing
but we learned from our fathers
let me try again

I'm sorry the _____ is gone
but I
let me try again

I'm sorry the _____ is _____
but we

I'm sorry
but

I

sorry

All the Signs Say

all the words tell us, sell us
something is ahead, stop on red
here to be fed, already made your bed
where you will lie, this is how to die
fill up the sky, put them up high
light and bright, everything is right
left at the sign, everything will be fine
check worry at the door, hurry no more
heaven in a basket, chicken in a casket
billions served a day, billions to pay
signs how to play, billboards how to pray
no escape you'll find, unless you go blind

Nature's Lowest Denominator

make monsters
from mammals
skull thick and hard
nightmare of a mouth
mandibles make mash
of bone and brain
feast on fear
find fault in fur
domesticate, deal death
cast man as king
lower the ladder
dominion's denominator

two sisters strong

one carried my nephews
until her belly bulged
two big for me to hug

one survived an overturned canoe
in frigid waters, doing all
she could to shield her son

one broke water
too soon, and held on for months
on her back in a hospital
protecting a miracle

they broke arms
in a mechanical exerciser bike
a fall from a tree
a shot from my leg cannon

they teach, they protect
bake and bike, ski and kayak
hunt and fish, gather and create

and because of them
I have nephews, nieces
love to give, to receive

I am lucky
I am two sisters strong

So Many Aprils

one hundred and fifty Aprils ago
at Appomattox
Generals sat apart
Grant's table, marble and square
and Lee at the front window,
his small, round

after so much bloodshed
they were civil, speaking first of
serving together in Mexico
small talk, before the moment
Grant penned the terms

the officers would keep their arms
and their horses

the war was over
but not the fight

it would take one hundred and fifty Aprils

the war, the fight
so many Aprils
while we waited
with the Prince
at the lake

for a swan to glissade

Élevé without the barre

Échappé and avant

do this ballet for us,
Copeland and Mack
become Odette and Sigfried

swan and prince
bring us your light
to a stage that has been
until today
dark

Ruling By Fractal

da Vinci saw the same
patterns in trees
wrote a rule for branches

I see these fractals, too
in history, how
like a birch we repeat

ten thousand years
of errors
over over over

from trunk to limb, limb
to branch, branch
to twig, twig to leaf

leaving nothing
left before

replication rules

Saved by Captain America

he held his small hands
on my cheeks and pressed
his own soft face against mine
are you sad, too?
why is mom sad?
my voice faltered on truth
we had to say goodbye
to a friend, I said
this is why we're sad

the tears held fast,
at the eyes' edge
my cheeks stayed dry
so his would

he is three and somehow
without words
I felt the need to shield him
from my sudden sorrow
I wanted to hug him close
let loose the flood, waiting

he reached for a book,
giving me an easy out

read to me?

he shifted to my lap
small fingers turning pages

away we went,
fighting with Captain America
and behind his broad shield
I hid from death

Return, Raven

now you play trickster
the cruelest of jokes
balls of earth into beauty
then bring the flood
and leave us alone
questioning your kind

return, Raven
remind us why
we are made of mud

The Three Year Old at Bedtime

plates pushing. crust colliding moltenmagma
earth enraged bubbling
boiling rapid
rising
tempest torrent seisimic storm eruption

explosion

aftermathashdustdebrisdetris
        disaster
                deathsadnesssorrow

Death By Social Media

you should have seen her Facebook
when she found out her Instagram had died
her world began to Tumblr
the beat of her heart reduced
to a twitter, just a Flickr
she couldn't Pinterest
the source of her pain
a dark Soundcloud followed
she no longer felt Linkedin
didn't write in her Livejournal
the Netflix of her life, reduced to cobwebs
without a Friendster
she felt herself Snapchat
she found only the Wordpress to write:
My life is over, there is no one to Yelp
then she wrapped a Lifeknot
around her Bebo
and jumped into Myspace

Death By Social Media, 2.0

he didn't like how her
Facebook turned
her status Twittered
And in an Instagram
she was with another Yahoo
and Hotmail
Walking Dead into
a House of Cards
his Lifelock was over
he would never trend again.
his only Pinterest?
setting the Match to Tinder
change his status to Explorer
and he set his selfie on Firefox
And Tumbler off
the Caring Bridge

Unbridled Progress

stand in shined shoes, derby hats
in black unbridled progress
ties and scarves wrapped tight
around your throat
as the noose on the moose
and your reins
on this land
the creatures
and her people

Two Hundred Years

I have swam beneath the ice for two hundred
winters
watched two hundred summer suns
shine upon this turbulent sea
saw your kin upon the shore
stepping gently, leaving only footprints
first, then wooden paddle strokes
soon rumbles and streaks in the sky

I have seen your rise
rapid as the moonlight spread across
a tundra plain, and now watch
while the moon-set makes ready
remembering how two hundred years
you watched for my spout
saw hope in the mist
made my grandmother into corsets
carved my mother for a mangled
meal for the bottom crawlers with
war weapons, steel whales
with your men sealed
screaming inside

some of your kind believe we
wield the ability to hear those
thoughts in your head, your actions
are already gale force, only if you listened
long enough at the ocean's edge
everything would crystalize
clear, and two hundred years
you would bear witness from sea

Field Trip to the Ghost House: Admit One

field trip across the river ice
but the concern had to do with theft and ghosts
and the elders were right, I admit

one room house, now gone
pilfered for firewood, rotted or stolen
I held onto the door frame

dinner still, on the table. Dust.
on the wall, seal skin boots
in the corner the black Victrola in anguish

This Was
(for Jane Hirshfield)

This was once life
before the bars and bars with bars
before gold was the color of love
when cheeks were red,
from teasing, not exposure
or vodka raining from plastic bottles

it remembers pulling on clothing
from the earth, feathers and scales
fur or skins

once, it was breakfast around
a fire-ring,
charred meat and family

once it longed for order,
plants grew in rows
wide eyed beasts in pens

it told them they needed more
rocks from the ground
were the real beauty

that was when it asked
for the bars
and they stepped inside

yes, it cides:

homo, sui, matri, patri, pest
settles on deicide

it will watch them topple
into the ditches and gutters
all, and then rise again

fireweed in the pavement cracks

Crocodile Killing Walrus

I believed the photo

a crocodile on an Alaskan beach
a hundred walrus hauled out
crowded in fear
the soft belly of one
flayed, contents spilled
foreign track to us in the sand
reptilian, new and ancient
all at once

I believed because I heard
the stories
saw the artifacts
painted creatures on kayaks
carved heads of monsters
crocodile, alligator, sinister
something not of this land
by a people of this land

they were not fools
10,000 years ago
this beast swam
while mammoth walked the shores

today, I was the fool

I believed

but only because I wanted
what we all want
the monsters
to sometimes not
be only human

Freedom in Chains

long ago we broke the links
connecting us to everything
found freedom in chains
conscience in captivity
man, beast, food — confined
control created confidence
future fitted for shackles

today we repair the links
connecting us to everything
captivity in conscience
confidence created control
confined — man, beast, food
fitted for future shackles
freedom found in chains

Coup Counts — for Chief Joe Medicine Crow

a single yellow feather
beneath his Army helmet
a Crow behind Nazi lines
counted coup on the enemy
sent hooves of fifty German horses
pounding off into the night

one hundred and three winters wise

a great uncle, White Man Runs Him, who wit-
nessed the chaos
people bathing in the Little Big Horn
then the cry of battle
women and children fleeing north
the camp beset with terror
history books forever distorted

they would stand for no more
the last of the great chiefs
made and killed, made and killed

now we are told again
the last of the great Chiefs are dead
as if the battle is finally over
and coup no longer counts

but let Chief Medicine Crow
take his long walk
let his words live
and know there is a young
Crow warrior somewhere
perhaps a great nephew
who will sneak into our enemy's camp
and steal their horses

teach us all again
what it means to be a chief

Death by Social Media 3.0

he needed an update
he'd watched his Prime expire
all the GoodReads were no longer Tinder for
his Kindle Fire
Pandora was open
he didn't have the emoticon
to Kickstart his iLife
he shared no Words with Friends
not even a PayPal
all sense of eHarmony was gone
not even Shazam or Alibaba
could save what was left
of his Google Earth

Guns in the English Classroom

Monday we discussed fragments
a Glock in my pocket

Tuesday was all commas
.44 on hip, .38 ankle, and .357
in a shoulder holster

Wednesday dangling participles
carrying a revolver on my hip

Thursday misplaced modifiers
packed a semi-auto with a smile

Friday was two, to, too
took two assault rifles to class, too

History

it's history, but
how can history be
the judge
if history is written by
the victors
and doomed to repeat history
the ones who don't learn

we're history
they're history
I'm history

the annals, the halls
the footsteps, the echoes
the ghosts, the mysteries

history is herstory
mystory, yourstory

history forgotten
history rewritten
revised, glamorized
romanticized, eulogized

history

is boring is exciting
is bloody
is dead white guys
is written in blood
dates names dates names
dusty, rusty, musty

can't rewrite
can't rewind
history is
was
will be

will

be

the weight of the immeasurable

the human heart

blood by the liter
liters of wine by the gallon
gallons of oil by the barrel
barrels of gold by the ounce
ounces of diamonds by the carat
carrots by the pound
pounding heart by beats per minute
in love and
love by no measurable means

Like Riding A Bike

like riding a bike, they say
but what about the first time
when age is one-part balance
and two parts fear and freedom
what is that like riding?

a bull?
a rocket?

like riding a bike, they say
but what about the last time
when age provides no freedom
from fear of balance
what is that like riding?

a bear?
a dragon?

After ANWR

Of course no one in New York was excited
when they discovered oil
beneath Central Park.

The various natives,
like the Manhatten Islanders,
the Bronxers and Harlemites
were concerned about the pigeons
and the homeless

their daily migration
from the park to the dumpsters,
would be disturbed by the drilling

the last of the reserves
in Texas, the gulf of Mexico, and Alaska
had long been sucked dry

the wild horses, the manatees, and the caribou
gone

The New Yorkers drew a line in the concrete
Central Park was sacred land

there would be no drilling there

not ever

Mosquito

I didn't even feel you
stick me
I didn't even know
you were draining me
slowly sucking
my love for life
my happiness
my sanity

still I didn't slap you
or swat you away
I grew accustomed to your
incessant hum
I grew to love your bite

you filled yourself
with the juice of my heart
and buzzed away
leaving me
with this solitary itch.

Not To Be

(thoughts after a student's suicide)

When I heard the news
I tried to picture her face in my mind's eye
eyes full of life igniting her precious visage
Ophelia's handful of flowers.

a dip into the sea of sorrows
swallows some,
turning cannons towards self-slaughter

perhaps I should have taught her
that some questions
are not
meant
to be
answered.

Simple Sauce

no cups of this or tablespoons
of that, only
olive oil and garlic
sea salt and hand ground pepper
this in a pan, medium heat
diced tomatoes, basil, oregano
a pinch of sugar, some grated carrot
more olive oil

while the dough rises
to marry the mixture
and sleep beneath a bed
of mozzarella and pepperoni

then into warm waiting oven

Tundra Prom

boutonnières and corsages shipped
four hundred miles at considerable expense
tuxedos sized and rented, deposits paid
hand delivered on the evening jet

a month's salary from evenings
after school at the grocery store
gone in a single night
"a night to remember" or whatever
the canned theme on frosted flutes

so much pomp when circumstances
couldn't be formal
high heals sticking in the mud
rubber boots and raincoats

for our photos at the dance
the three of us posed
like Hollywood action stars
guns and a samurai sword

kids dressed up like rich adults
pretending to be something
we would never know

They say...

men need
women know
boys think
girls learn
babies understand
cats fear
dogs like

they say
they say
they say

say, who
are they?

why do
we always
believe what
they say?

Before the Avalanche

before hell cracked loose
far above
and darkened our world
an apology, a revelation
the rising mountain
between us, fell away

before the white wall of snow
barreled toward us
we shared a moment
that would keep me alive

long after
we were first
swallowed, then beaten
buried

long after
I washed out
below, broken, battered
bruised

long after
you appeared, disappeared
again and again

long after
we fell, and the first night
fell, haunting
and each thereafter

what came before
the avalanche
tore us apart
forever carries me
over each mountain

Old Wounds and Flaws

my eyes don't see
the world the same
they are dirty brown
I see that
I know that
my hair, too
brown, but the eyes
in certain shades
see other colors
the wrong colors
some might say

then the scars
a thin white line
on the left palm
running midway
from ring finger
to the center
on the wrist, broken twice
another scar, red and thick
on the knee joint,
not a slice from barbed wire and football, but a
box knife
in a grocery store

broken this and that
tailbone
ribs
funny bone

old wounds and flaws
on the surface
all stories
inside something else
a mystery, even to me

SEER

seeking the future
a crystal ball in your palm
the world upside down

The Rising Leaves

crinkling and cackling as they swirl
zombie leaves take form
rise from the dead and dirt
raging against life
lifting into the sky
once more towards trees
that once held them
loved them, discarded them
with winter and so much
spring sun budding anew
break the bows
tears the trunks
uproot the unkind

Unbecoming Man

the trees tremble
wind
the robin sings
warning
the hare freezes
fear
the bear stands
dominance
we become stone
diminutive

Earth Day

one is not enough
for this planet we call home
we can do better

Ghost Ride

after the first
scratches, dings
dirt and rust

when you can
pedal hard, and
at the last moment
jump free
kick your feet
and let go

into the lake
off a bluff, over
a riverbank
down your street

understand this:
some day
your bike will
keep rolling

Tiring

don't tread on me

tired

worn thin
blown out
punctured
and out of balance

tired

slick, slow leak
low pressure
I am rubber
on this road

tired

overinflated, misaligned
cracked, flat
slashed, burned

I'm tired

Monster Mine

at the mining protest, the boy
who protests everything
from bedtime to breakfast
points to a problem
the parents and other people
have missed
the adults concern themselves
with pollution and wild salmon
habitat loss and toxins
his concern runs deeper
into the mystery, and what
we're willing to risk
slips deep into
the heart of the lake

the mine can't go in
he protests,
it will kill the lake monster!

Presidential

you, Sir, have destroyed
both the office and the word

the origin is Latin, not that you care,

origins have no bearing
on a compass with no needle

praesident meant:
sitting before

as in, your job was to sit
at the head of our country's table
say grace, be graceful
act with dignity, not Hannity

definitions of this word
include terms antithetical
to your very being:
dignified, stately
composure that befits
a president

it is no wonder,
presidential will join
the obsolete term:
presiding, watching over
as this comfort is also gone

inside the very word
presidential: present
preside, reside

you see only side and I
an illusion, No Collusion!

your gold gilded towers
lean towards treason
Fake News! we lose
reason and rule of law
you mock, turned
the bully pulpit, to shit
Sad!

Dog People

we spent millennia taming wolves
selecting for gentle demeanors
soft features and loyalty
now?
a dog for everything

show dogs, sled dogs
guard dogs, guide dogs
hot dogs, stray dogs
corn dogs, Shar Pei dogs
dog eared, dog leg
dog eat dog, doggie bag
sun dog, lost dog
big dog, bird dog
fire dog, boon dog
sick as a dog, coon dog
dog gone, dog song
dog day, dog play
bad dog, mad dog
doggie smile, dog pile

dog this, dog that
all but a dog cat

Shards and Chandeliers

we amble down the dirt road in the morning
sun, her little feet stomp on the thin ice cover-
ing clear puddles, the crystal coatings shards
and chandeliers spray from beneath her tiny
soles, she shrieks with what life fills my exis-
tence in a way I didn't know possible and I be-
come a puddle at the thought of her world ever
shattering without me there at her side

On This Day in History

Lincoln takes a bullet the same day
the Titanic hits the iceberg
Webster's dictionary a day before
Samuel Johnson published
his and Wild Bill
became sheriff

the day before Ray Kroc
started McDonalds
Davinci gave his first cry
and after Tiger
won his first Masters
and Thomas Jefferson
was born

the bullet and the iceberg
each struck the same day
death followed a day later

everything we think
we know happened
everything we know
happened we think

Arctic War(n/m)ing

melting permafrost
sinkholes open to reveal
the past as future

Listen and Learn

I swung her around to my back
clasp my hands together
beneath her little bottom
squatted, grabbed the dog leash
turned toward home

her little cartoon chatter
skipped from colors and mountains
I like to ride piggy back and
trees, rocks, funny puppy
big truck, listen to the water
where is momma?
and next time
I'll travel with her on the airplane
—somewhere between it all —
she said: I see a big fat moose

my mind scrolled back through
her rambling and struck on:
Big Fat.
I didn't like her saying that.
Wondered where she heard
such an insensitive phrase
I was ready for the talk
with her brother

"Where did you hear that?"
I asked

right there!
her little arm shot out
a pointing finger

then movement in the alders
half again the length
of the dog leash away
uncomfortably close

a big fat moose

psychopomp *(psuchopompos)*

for five days
a gray wolf slept
curled at her grave
the guide of her soul
or a secret friend
met berry picking

the people mourned her
sometimes imagined
soft sounds of the child
they tucked in her parka

on the sixth day
a round depression
in the snow
wolf and woman tracks

leading away

This Crystal Ball

exactly how a crystal ball
reveals the future
eludes me

the present is inverted
through a glass sphere

there are theories
of other worlds
planes and dimensions
the theory of mind

so many theories

perhaps seeing myself
in a mirror upside down
will reveal as much
about the future
as my little brain
can handle

the medicine rises

the medicine rises
water becomes a ghost
from the rocks
air becomes fire
as a thousand snakes
sing in unison
spirits slip inside
demons drip drop
cleansed by fire
cleansed by water
the medicine rises

the snow tells stories

here a snow shoe hare
took his last jump
the lynx left crimson clumps
and two unlucky feet
then crept off

there dainty round
fox prints skirting
the dwarf hemlock
barely leaving a mark
then a straight line
toward the ghost
of a ptarmigan wing
pressed into the snow
and three white feathers
flecked with blood

the wolverine's character
is never betrayed
lone line of round dimples
and claws cut the cornice
his tracks spell intent

between all this
two lines, sometimes four
our ski tracks, meandering
up the valley to the frozen lakes
our marks in the snow
leave a different story
one that is still being written

thinking of you

I am stuck in traffic
a line of cars
ahead for miles
all at a stand still
peaceful snow fall, though

radio on
interesting interview

sorry I
won't make it home
in time to help
put the kids to bed

the truth

of the matter
the truth
is out there
the truth
when you know
the truth
don't want to hear
the truth
there is no
the truth
tell the
the truth
is hidden
the truth
is a fruit
the truth
speak
the truth
look for
ask for
half truth
absolute truth
the truth
hurts
the truth
prevails

Message Sent

in the time of carrier pigeons
wings carried messages
the writer contemplated
weather and whether the bird
might encounter a raptor
a flash from a shotgun muzzle
the message becoming
ticker tape confetti

carrier pigeons have flown
wi-fi carries messages
the writer's contempt
whether or weather
raptor like rapture
in a flash
the blast
the message is lost
only if it is never sent

On the Fence

once you commit
to crossing
there is no going back

barbed wire requires
certain care
look at a leather couch
or my left palm
those thin scars come easy
but heal hard

pole fences appear
easy to climb
but wood rots
nails rust and betray
everything tumbles down

stone, steal, concrete
all this division of
land, labor, love

build a wall
around your heart
and then, when
you find yourself
on the fence

don't linger

Dead Horse Trail

defined by horsepower
cannot rein in desire
ridden to death
ends justify being mean

this work horse
this dark horse
cantered, loped, galloped
rode hard and put away
to whet our appetite

barn sour, behind the bit
buck and crib
sired a sound
rogue stallion
we cannot put down

and we leave in our wake
a trail rutted and rotten

Missing: Socks

the mystery of modern man
with all his technological wonders
this simple solution eluded humanity
there was no device
gizmo or gadget

everyone endured
no one asked
wondered or investigated
the disappearances
troubled so few
others too shy to complain
some simply embarrassed

the status quo
never questioned

and the socks escaped
one by one by one

Cutting Caribou

cutting caribou
smile with each slice
a gift from the Arctic
cuts to the bone
this realization
happiness brought
in a bag
the tundra missed
like an old friend

Today, Refused

the note from his teacher

got carried away
today, refused
said
said
said

words that blurred

read and read again

said said said
even the word: *said*
began to make no sense

World of Birds

at this moment
the world belongs to birds
in the distance gulls
crying out with joy
as they circle an ocean of trash
a chickadee flutters at the feeder
a woodpecker taps at tallow
an unknown bird squeaks
like new shoes on a basketball court
these creatures within arms reach

in the birch and spruce
small songbirds singing

orbiting over this all
raptors and ravens
three eagles, a hawk

and from the coop
the chickens
cluck and call out warnings
enemies in the sky
enemies in the woods
enemies in the ground

a man-made bird flies through
all falls still for a second
except for the gulls
then a raven caws
birds sing

but the chickens
remain silent

Empty Nest

we take family walks
rain or shine, through the woods
around the neighborhood
up the mountain

today my son caught fish
in potholes deep enough
to hide halibut and king salmon
stingrays and colossal squid

sometimes we find treasures
silver lug nut
homemade tent stake
rocks with veins of quartz

today we stopped at a ruined hive
high in the tree
took turns throwing rocks
until it fell to the snow

we examined the empty nest
paper thin comb
no honey, much
to his disappointment

it would have tasted good
in the king salmon salad
he cooked as we ambled home
back to our own little nest

Listen

listen
you can hear your heart

listen
animals will speak

listen
walls are no obstacle

listen
water whispers become roars

listen
trails call to you

listen
ancient spirits sing

listen
again to your heart

Political Decorum

burned by midnight oil
tongues and pockets greased
bacon and loin drippings
one-two-many cocktails

straight shooters and oysters
tables of agendas
politics around poles
poll dances with death
discriminating cases
incriminating tastes
legalese for legal ease
party for the partisan
no budget for this bill

The Shaman Girl

in eighth grade
I met a shaman
this girl possessed
the power
of kindness
my magical friend
transformed me
changed the skin
others saw
so I was no longer
different, strange
decades later
when I felt scared, again
she knew
the shaman sent me
Raven skin
then
Salmon skin
with her gift
transformed, no longer
afraid to be
different, strange

Girl Made Climate Change

with your arrival
a sea change
initially some resistance
skepticism calved, caved
glacier blue eyes
melted the ice
the climate changed
our world warmed

Red Blue

funny how they would
have us divided

each heartless

red   blue

veins and arteries
half leading towards
the remaining away
each relying on chambers

pressure too high

ablation, aphasia, artificial
donors, draws, diastolic

funny how they would
have us forget this

we are indivisible
we bleed

   love

This I Miss

my daughter calls Covid
"the sickness"
and I am sad for her
not getting to play
with friends, but it doesn't
phase her — though
says she misses Taco King
and Joe's cats

our friends miss going to movies
sitting in a restaurant
bellying up to a bar
sporting events, live music
books stores and birthdays
pools and playgrounds
cookouts and camping

what do I miss?

not worrying
about the awkward
space between us

breakfast at a cafe

hugs

The Treasure Hunters

we hunted for treasures
along the banks of rivers
the Missouri in Montana
Alaska's Kuskokwim

bits and pieces of buffalo bone
bird skulls and broken arrowheads
mammoth ivory, shell casings

we once dug a dozen holes
in the corral, searching for poker chips
relics our parents hid as kids
we never found their stash
didn't stumble upon lost loot
a stagecoach robbed

my eyes still search
and I send my own kids
on hunts

they will discover
the true treasure
can never collect dust
on a shelf, enriched by
memories of dirty hands
thirst, and shared imagination

Lügenpresse

I could barely breathe
blue sky, bird song
pea gravel crunching beneath my soles
Dachau's wrought iron gate
three haunting words:
Arbeit macht frei
a bold-faced lie
one of so many the Nazis would spin

inside the camp
I walked the path of the imprisoned
in the shunting room
where the prisoners turned over their posses-
sions
shaved, disinfected, and showered
I learned of this term: lügenpresse

as if the horrors of that place
weren't enough
a subtle warning to us all
until Hitler grabbed the reins
of German media
reporters were the lügenpresse
then, after Kristallnacht
the foreign press – lügenpresse!
which included American media

I left Dachau in pieces
threw coins in the gold creek outside the gate
hoping for something better
wishing it away, wondering

are we all outside that gate now?
our own president – undignified, indignant
pointing, lying, yelling

fake news!
fake news!
fake news!

Zoom ™

infected nation
everyone making lame jokes
about no pants
cats and dogs
and the kids.

oh, the complaints about kids
virtual backgrounds
pajamas and bad hair
bedrooms and bathrooms
weird walls and —
ZOOM BOMB!

new words for a brave new world
Zoom. Zooming. Zoomed.

All Zoomed out.

Soothing Souls

hand crafted warmth
from a friend, for my love
to carry her beyond this cancer
like a doctor or a shaman
he is today's fixer
spotted seal skin slippers
trimmed in black
purple, white, magenta
iridescent beaded snowflakes
a single red bead reminder
perfection --- was creation
seal soothing soles
seal soul soothing

ESKIMO BASEBALL

I remember when Benny
stole my baseball glove

he and the other boys
raced off, down the muddy boardwalk
laughter fading with distance
my soft leather mitt
clutched in his hand

they probably had never
touched a baseball glove
before that cool spring day

the irony
didn't occur to me then
as I choked back the tears

I was the only white boy
in the village

kass'aq!

the only left-hander, too.

Spring Change

after we finished shoveling
slush and dog turds
his mom, inside on the couch
recovering from chemo

I showed him how to cut a milk jug, a makeshift
oil pan
grab the sockets, some rags
where is the funnel?
there, bring that
set it here, watch out, careful
we opened the Honda's drain plug

he worried when he saw
my hand coated in black

will you be okay, Dad?

I'll be okay, Son. *We'll* be okay.

For the Essentials

there will be no medals for you
no dinners in your honor, no book offers
movies deals, or dramas
capturing your sacrifices
your sweat and toil
for a nation hungry
for chocolate ice cream
and extra toilet paper
essentials we purchase

delivered, unboxed, stocked, bagged

no pension to lose
no sick leave
no funeral fund
or insurance — against anything

know this, you heroes
your selflessness
does not go unnoticed

and after the cleanup
on aisle America
is over
we will find a away

to give you the thanks
you have earned

I'm Just Saying

I sorta used
the last
sheet left on
the roll
and realize
you would have
done
the same
I'd apologize
but one sheet
wasn't enough
and so, yeah—

Uncertain Endings

the play is the thing we return to
and we know what is coming
how it ends
but hope for a twist

as if we could learn
alongside the characters
transform ourselves, too
live again, night after night

uncertain endings for all
a curtain call
we cannot live expecting tragedy
but we all have our tickets

Last Poem

I can't help but wonder
about our last poem
humanity's very final
thought captured in verse
handwritten or typed
scrawled in desperation
upon a wall
pencil or pen
pensively or sudden flash
of inspired ink?

will our final poem
have a rhyme scheme
or be about a scheme
rhythm and organized
or offbeat and offbeat

audience of one
the death of many
famine or flames
drowning or drought

future or lost love?

poetry itself:
language and emotion
lost to ones and zeroes?

And this final poem
this last poem of humankind ---
will the poet know
the weight of those words